2016

"Happy Birthday"

Love,
Shirl

Friendship
Is a Journey

Blue Mountain Arts®

New and Best-Selling Titles

By Susan Polis Schutz:
To My Daughter with Love on the Important Things in Life
To My Son with Love

By Douglas Pagels:
Always Remember How Special You Are to Me
Required Reading for All Teenagers
The Next Chapter of Your Life
You Are One Amazing Lady

By Marci:
Angels Are Everywhere!
Friends Are Forever
10 Simple Things to Remember
To My Daughter
To My Granddaughter
To My Mother
To My Son
You Are My "Once in a Lifetime"

By Wally Amos, with Stu Glauberman:
The Path to Success Is Paved with Positive Thinking

By Minx Boren:
Friendship Is a Journey
Healing Is a Journey

By Carol Wiseman:
Emerging from the Heartache of Loss

Anthologies:
A Daybook of Positive Thinking
A Son Is Life's Greatest Gift
Dream Big, Stay Positive, and Believe in Yourself
Girlfriends Are the Best Friends of All
God Is Always Watching Over You
The Love Between a Mother and Daughter Is Forever
Nothing Fills the Heart with Joy like a Grandson
There Is Nothing Sweeter in Life Than a Granddaughter
There Is So Much to Love About You... Daughter
Think Positive Thoughts Every Day
Words Every Woman Should Remember
You Are Stronger Than You Know

Friendship Is a Journey

A Celebration of True Connection and Deep Caring

Minx Boren, MCC

Blue Mountain Press™

Boulder, Colorado

Dedication

To a lifetime of friends. Each of you has taught me, in your own unique way, to love deeply and unconditionally, to delight in living, to laugh at all the ways life does not go according to plan, and to savor all the precious moments along the way.

Library of Congress Catalog Card Number: 2015043418
ISBN: 978-1-59842-981-7

Printed in China.
First Printing: 2016

This book is printed on recycled paper.

This book is printed on paper that has been specially produced to be acid free (neutral pH) and contains no groundwood or unbleached pulp. It conforms with the requirements of the American National Standards Institute, Inc., so as to ensure that this book will last and be enjoyed by future generations.

Library of Congress Cataloging-in-Publication Data

Names: Boren, Minx, author.
Title: Friendship is a journey : a celebration of true connection and deep caring / Minx Boren.
Description: Boulder, Colorado : Blue Mountain Arts, 2016.
Identifiers: LCCN 2015043418 | ISBN 9781598429817 (paperback)
Subjects: LCSH: Friendship. | Interpersonal relations. | BISAC: FAMILY & RELATIONSHIPS / General. | FAMILY & RELATIONSHIPS / Friendship.
Classification: LCC BJ1533.F8 B7145 2016 | DDC 158.2/5--dc23
LC record available at http://lccn.loc.gov/2015043418

Blue Mountain Arts, Inc.
P.O. Box 4549, Boulder, Colorado 80306

Table of Contents

Introduction

Someone wise once said that there are three kinds of friends... those who enter into our lives for a season, a reason, or a lifetime. No matter the way or why someone special appears on our life's path, our lives are changed somehow because of their presence. Thinking back, I can recall friends who showed up for a while, embellishing and enlivening a certain time, place, or experience, only to take their leave as we each moved on in new directions. Then there were those who appeared serendipitously just when I needed their companionship or perspective or capacity to be fully present and understanding.

I remember most fondly the friends who have been around the longest and made the journey through years of ups and downs and perhaps even going around in circles. These are the friends whose phone numbers are embedded in my mind (or at least on my speed dial). They are the first ones I think of when I need a lift or a sanity check or simply time out with a favorite playmate. And they might be the very last person on my mind when I go to sleep... sending them loving well wishes or including them in my prayers.

My friends are very important to me. They add a measure of sweetness to whatever I am doing, and they bring meaning to my life. They light up my days and comfort me during the dark nights and difficult times. I feel so deeply blessed by all those who have befriended me through the peaks and valleys of my life—those who have offered me their understanding and their wisdom, a place at their tables and the shirts off their backs, and whatever else might be needed.

This book was written with my friends in mind, and my hope is that you will share it with your friends—those who have journeyed with you along life's highways and byways to this point in time.

In the spirit and adventure of it all,

— Minx

friendship is a journey
it begins with that first passing glance
or unexpected encounter
or lovely introduction
or random pairing

a few casual words perhaps
or a meaningful exchange
if time and occasion permit
and some spark of interest
or curiosity or commonality
ignites and takes hold

then sometimes days or weeks
or even years later
we might look back and marvel
at the miraculous beginnings
of this ever-deepening bond
connecting us one to the other
through highs and lows
and everything in between
times of such lightness of being
that every moment glittered
with joy and promise
as well as those of such heaviness
or sorrow that only our firm and loyal grip
kept one or the other from sinking

friendship grows
moment by moment
kindness by kindness
shared steps
along both easy and rocky terrains
all of it integral to the gratifying
and lasting bond that forges
deep and fulfilling relationships

no matter where we travel
or the wonders we get to see
friendship remains one of the great
journeys of any lifetime

The Gift of True Friendship

Friends are mirrors where we can see ourselves more clearly reflected. They hold a welcoming space for the whole of us—our great gifts and strengths as well as our foolishness and foibles. They are compassionate toward our fears and past failings, but their focus remains steadfast on reminding us of who we are now and the possibilities here before us. Henry David Thoreau speaks of friends as those who "cherish each other's hopes... are kind to each other's dreams." There is no more gracious offering in all the world.

It is said that friends are the family we choose for ourselves. As a dear friend of mine wisely observed, it is not necessarily bonds of blood that link a family, but rather ties of respect and the intimacy born of communal experiences and exchanges of ideas and more. It is in the great good company of friends that we can show up whole and unfeigned, without the need for either pretense or posturing. We do not have to measure our words or measure up to some elusive standard. True friendship is the ultimate treasure we gift ourselves simply by making time and opening our hearts to another.

*t*rue and forever friends we are
how could we be otherwise
so entwined are the stories
of our journeys
that they blur at the edges
of whose good idea or silly
scheme it was that sparked
this or that cherished moment
now revisited as we curl up
together on the comfy couch
warming ourselves
with the kindling of memories
all the while creating a cozy haven
to cradle new dreams

kindred spirits
in each other's eyes
we see reflected back
our best selves held sacred
heart to heart
protected from doubts
by the vigilance of our shared
love and appreciation

chosen companions
leaning on each other
in the quiet room and in life
feeling our tenderness
toward each other expand
to embrace the world

I am your friend—
it's as simple and as complex as that
our friendship has a life all its own
that is bigger than you or me alone

sometimes it's all fun and laughter—
a shopping spree or time spent
wandering and wondering together
and sometimes it's about facing a challenge
hand in hand

and so it goes—
this flow of giving and receiving
of love and support
and everything else
that makes this friendship real

you are my friend—
it's as delightful and important as that
this simple declaration
has a reach and magnitude greater
than either of us can know
and so it is
that we are both so blessed

Counting My Blessings

For years now, each night before going to bed,
I write down what I am most grateful for: three
specific, good things that happened that day. From
time to time, I read through my gratitude journal
as a way to remind myself of the goodness of my
days. What I am noticing is that, year after year,
my entries have to do mostly with these two
things: the time I have spent in the good company
of my Self, either relaxing in quiet contemplation
or doing some physical movement, and the time I
have spent in the good company of others.

I cannot imagine my life without all the special
REALationships that light up my days and comfort
me during the dark nights and difficult times. I feel
so deeply blessed by all those who have befriended
me throughout my life. They have offered me their
time and compassion, shared their knowledge and
expertise, and have proffered handshakes or hugs,
lists of instructions, letters of recommendation,
as well as valid praise along with valuable,
constructive guidance.

*No words can ever quite
convey the rich complexity
of emotions that give REALationships
both substance and sustainability*

*no words can adequately express
the vibrant connection
experienced by even the simplest
exchange of devoted friends
whose bond is allowed to blossom
in the spaciousness
of time and tenderness*

*loyal camaraderie is a sweet and
serendipitous miracle we can only attract
by being who and how we are
with neither pretense nor airs
for only in the rarified atmosphere
of deep authenticity and unfettered
understanding
can friendship take hold and flourish*

*like lush tree branches reaching to the gift of sky
so do REALationships gravitate toward the light
of loving kindness
gesture by generative gesture
whether smiles or tears
shared laughter or deep concern
each freely offered
and appreciatively received*

there is no other way

It's those extra
ordinary small things
that you do with neither
fuss nor fanfare
that touch my heart

it's those unexpectedly
simple and sincere gestures
that you offer with
so much kindness and caring
that inspire my appreciation

it's those exquisitely
precious sweet moments
when you reach out
to extend a helping hand
or to share in my joy
that stir my soul

my heart is filled with gratitude
and in this moment
all I can say is thank you
for the blessing of your friendship

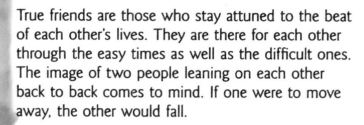

Friends Are There
for Each Other

True friends are those who stay attuned to the beat of each other's lives. They are there for each other through the easy times as well as the difficult ones. The image of two people leaning on each other back to back comes to mind. If one were to move away, the other would fall.

This notion of staying closely connected and involved in the daily rhythm of the life of another is one that is dear to me. Over the years I have developed various practices for being in touch. With some friends who live far away, we have learned to schedule weekly phone visits so as to always be present to one another. With others who live closer by, beyond the e-mails and check-in calls, it might be a monthly lunch or movie or women's circle. With still others, the rhythm might be more sporadic while we nonetheless remain committed to connecting with one another in some ongoing way.

I cannot respond to the need of another if I don't know there is one. Nor can they be there for me if I am not willing to impart with complete honesty where exactly I am at any point in time. Keeping up with friends and staying in the loop of each other's lives has become an essential practice that I cherish.

*f*riends share...
recipes and potlucks; sugar, eggs, butter,
and leftovers
special secrets, sacred memories,
sweet dreams
good news, trying times, rough patches
real life, reliable remedies, quiet respites
good will, good stories, good books
hope, happiness, and spontaneous laughter

friends offer...
warmth, comfort, meaningful moments
time, talents, treasures
concern, advice, perspective, wisdom
the missing tool or expertise to fix the leak,
ease the logjam, or accept the loss
a deep well from which to draw sustenance
and support
love, love, and more love

friends are...
the bedrock on which we can stand tall
the anchor we can trust to hold us firm
the advocate we can count on when the
going gets tough
the cheerleader we can rely on to keep us
motivated and on track
the companion we can turn to
in sadness or celebration
an irreplaceable gift that immeasurably
enriches everything

Friends Show Up

One of the most wonderful gifts of staunch friendships is the way that we show up for each other year after year for all sorts of reasons—special occasions and non-occasions alike, fun-filled festivities, difficult challenges, or heartbreaking tragedies. We do so without fanfare and without keeping tabs or expecting anything in return, except the gift of each other's presence.

Years ago I needed two total hip replacements. The surgeries were scheduled three months apart. My friend Barbara, who happens to be a nurse, lives three thousand miles away, yet she chose to show up for both surgeries—keeping me company, caring for me, and even spending the nights in a sleeping bag spread out on the floor of my hospital room in order to stay by my side. I cannot begin to tell you the difference it made to my spirits and my recovery. Then, too, there were all the friends who showed up with food, flowers, favorite books, or other carefully chosen gifts to demonstrate their love through their kindness and concern, each facilitating my healing process in their own way.

Beyond these angelic companions, there were others who flew long distances to take turns helping me along at home for the first month following each surgery while my ability to do things for myself was severely limited. As it turned out, the whole experience became one of love and connection.

More recently, I took a turn serving as president of a local organization. The roll-up-your-sleeves support and outstanding wise counsel I received from more than a dozen dedicated colleagues, each of whom I consider my friend, made all the difference in what I was able to accomplish during the three years I served in an executive capacity. They made me look good. Friends graciously do that for us!

Actually, *graciously* and *gracefully* are perfect descriptive words to highlight the qualities that friends bring with them when they arrive on the scene. It's not simply about responsibility or duty. It's about grace and goodness and genuine concern.

We have all experienced the generosity of spirit that is woven into sincere acts of caring. And we have all had the opportunity to show up for others in the same way. I dare say that many of the most satisfying and memorable encounters in our lives involve this capacity to be of service to one another on this journey called life.

friends show up
not because they should
not because they must
but because of the magnitude
of love
because of the magnetic
force of compassion

friends show up
because they can
because life
has come knocking
and they are there
to answer
now
not when or then
but in the immediate
potency of the call

friends show up
not because it is time
or timely
not because it is easy
or tough
smooth or rough
not because it is
reasonable or not
but because this is
what matters
now
no matter what is next

friends show up
because it feels right
and real
because it makes
their hearts sing
or sob
because it might ache
or break
if they did not
because joy lives
in their being present
and of service
when you need them
most

friends just show up

A Friend in Need and a Friend in Deed

I heard of the concept of "a friend in need and a friend in deed" through Marcia Levy and Susan Lubin who live in Texas. When Susan was diagnosed with cancer, Marcia showed up day and night to support her through her treatment as well as through the whole healing process. We have all heard stories about good friends being there for each other, and they always warm our hearts. What makes this story remarkable is that after Susan was well on the road to full recovery, she and Marcia (both wives of doctors with quick access to excellent care) decided that it would be wonderful if other women in their city could receive the kind of immediate and intensive care that was available to Susan. And so together they raised millions of dollars and were instrumental in the creation of the Seton Breast Care Center in Austin. The two were architects of the programs and services offered and ensured that the state-of-the-art center had the look and feel of a spa. Being inspired by each other, they did whatever it took (and it took a lot!) to make it happen. Such is the power of Friendship (with a capital F).

A friend "in deed" is indeed a special kind of friend, showing up when others disappear or fall away. It is these times of great need that separate loyal and substantive friendships from those that are just about fun and fluff.

Your kindness arrived
at just the perfect moment
and it caught me by sweet surprise
just before I could have tumbled into an abyss
I had not seen spreading all around me

your concern came calling
beckoning me back from
the edge of my sadness and
like an offering of honeyed tea
quenched my thirst for something
that could soothe my weary and worried heart

your loving presence showed up
and offered a magical balm
of comfort and caring that spread
across my being in the wake
of your tender reaching out
soothing the uncertainty and doubt
that had occupied all too much
of my narrowed attention

and there at the center
of your enveloping love
as your warmth melted away
my frozen fears and your voice
quieted my bluesy bouts of despondence
was the unimagined blessing
of peace and hope and on their wings
the strength to carry on

Each Friend Is
Unique and Precious

I have a string of prayer beads. Each bead is different and unique and represents someone special in my life. There are times when I like to sit quietly and just run the beads through my fingers one by one as a way to bless and give thanks for each precious companion who has walked with me at some point in my life journey. This simple practice not only connects me to those significant people, but it feeds my soul.

The Chinese calligraphic symbol for *friend* is that of a lake upon another lake. It is meant to express the harmony that can happen when these two entities join together in order to refresh and replenish each other. Such is the revitalizing effect that friends can offer us.

I heard a story about a young child who was asked, "What is a friend?" The child responded that when you have a friend, "your name is safe in their mouth." That phrase resonates with me. Faithful friends are not only wonderful companions and cheerleaders, but also loyal advocates who always speak to and about each other with love and respect. They stand firm and tall as a *no gossip zone,* where only appreciative comments and encouraging thoughts are allowed.

Ours is a friendship
that spans the years
like a multitude of bridges
both grand and small
our sharing and caring
have woven cables strong enough
to offer safe passage across
the deep crevasses and roiling
waters of life

then, too, there are the great
joys and grand vistas
we have experienced
in each other's good company
across the miles and milestones
of our long journey
to this vantage point
in time

and so as I stand here now
thinking of you
may my love and appreciation
span the rainbow bridge
from my heart to yours
as I celebrate you in all your
magnificent wholeness

Friends Listen Generously

One of the greatest gifts friends can give to each other is to simply be there to listen with neither judgments nor agenda. The straightforward act of turning toward each other with a generosity of spirit and time is a priceless gesture of caring.

Real listening requires both ears, both eyes, and a whole lot more. But in our very busy lives, where multitasking is lauded and everything clamors for our attention at once, real listening can become a forsaken art. Here are some ways friends sincerely honor each other by listening:

Friends listen with their eyes. They make eye contact and watch gestures, body language, and facial expressions for subtle keys to deeper understanding.

Friends listen with their ears open. They do not selectively listen, but are fully there for each other. They listen not only to the words being said, but also to the nuances of what is being conveyed—the whole of it.

Friends listen with their minds and hearts. They don't have preconceived ideas or opinions, and they are able to put aside any biases, filters, and narrow frames of reference in order to be fully engaged with what you are saying. They keep their minds open, even if they disagree or are impatient about what they are hearing. And they pay attention beyond the facts to what their hearts sense, feel, and know.

Friends are genuinely interested in what you have to say. They are curious and want to know more about you, as well as discover what you can teach them.

Friends allow for silence. Silence is a gift that is given—a respectful pause for information to be received, absorbed, and processed and for questions to be carefully formed.

Friends listen attentively. They are willing to set aside their own thoughts and ready answers and stop inwardly formulating and rehearsing their responses so they can reply to what is present in the moment.

Friends consider what it would be like to be you. They want to understand how it would feel to walk around in your shoes and to have arrived at this point in your life journey.

Through the generous gift of listening, friends are truly present to one another. It takes time, but authentic friendships blossom in the spaciousness of good listening.

On those gray days
when sadness threatens
to obscure all hope
and block all possibility
it is you I turn to and
I am never disappointed

on bright shiny days
when life is good and
opportunities are flowing my way
it is you I turn toward
to share my news and rejoice with me

with an open heart and mind
you offer me solace or celebration
respectful advice or exuberant congratulations
unbridled encouragement or easy acceptance

it is this special quality of loving presence
that you demonstrate so easily and
selflessly that I so appreciate
and have learned to rely on

you are my all-weather friend

It was an extraordinary ordinary lunch
made especially delicious
by the eagerness we felt
to be in each other's company
sharing both delightful trifles
and the more substantial fare of
deep concerns and closely-held dreams

it was an experience to savor
made rich and pungent by our commitment
to show up whole and undistracted by all else
that could vie for our attention or interfere
with this scrumptious time of connection

our willingness to listen generously
as we each presented morsel by morsel
our most real truths
and the oh-so-satisfying stories
we gladly offered to one another all added
to the banquet of our togetherness

it was difficult to distinguish whether
the appreciative nods and sighs of satisfaction
were in honor of the food or the array of
carefully articulated thoughts in the pleasure
of each other's company
and, oh, the sweet stories we shared along with
the chocolate espresso torte
nothing could have been more satisfying
and so we agreed of course

same time next year

Friends Share Their
Stories

Our stories matter. Since the dawn of civilization, people have entertained each other and shared their lives through the telling of stories. Ordinary occurrences recalled around the campfires of long ago enabled our ancestors to transmit knowledge and information, to build relationships, and to make sense of the world around them. By recounting our history we bring greater meaning and significance to our experiences, capturing and validating the essence of what it is to be human.

Whether we narrate or write or draw or sing our stories, our sharing can bring clarity and context to the seemingly random events of our lives. It can provide an opportunity to complete and let go of certain versions of ourselves that no longer serve us and keep us locked in the past, including those experiences that can cause pain to our physical and psychic being. The telling of our stories can inspire us to tackle our own fears and challenges. It gives us the courage to face adversity and reach beyond the limitations that confront or confound us.

Our stories provide a legacy that can instruct, influence, and inspire those around us as well as countless others miles away. Several years ago, my cousin Howie and I spent several days sitting on his back deck "interviewing" each other and giving voice to some of our especially personal memories while simultaneously recording our exchange on video. Howie's parents had both died when he was a child, and he felt the need to tell his story so that if he, too, died young, his children would still be able to know about his life, his ideas and ideals, as well as what he valued most. I was there because I was about to undergo two major surgical procedures and wanted to create a legacy for my son and perhaps his future offspring... just in case. Looking back, we would both say this bearing witness to each other was a most amazing and powerful experience.

We as humans experience most of our encounters through words. It is through our conversations and stories that people get to know us and know about us. So it makes good sense to pay attention to exactly what we are saying, how our words color our experiences, and how they impact the way we see and are seen in the world.

Is there anything more precious
than the gift of a story
one that still lives in the soul
of the teller

no matter how it is shaped
and reshaped
through the shifting lens
of time and space
the experience still rings true

your words float toward me
as you thoughtfully shape
and gather them into a gift
offering me first one harmonious
chord of your journey song
and then another

I sit here quietly
almost holding my breath
lest I disturb even a single word
before it has found its rightful tone
and timbre
and landed safely in my heart

and so it is that I come to know
those who have birthed you
loved you
taught and inspired you

and so it is that I, too, experience
your journey
as we relive your story together

the clock ticks on
and I, too, offer you some notes
of my story-song
as I form into words
some of my most precious memories

and so it is that turn by turn
we search and sift
through dusty recollections
and shiny moments when
we have each glimpsed
life's secret treasures
and have been awakened
and transformed

and in the afterglow
of these illuminating
intimacies I sit here
awestruck by an expanded
awareness of not only your life
but of life itself
as your story becomes a part of me
as it weaves its way
into my knowingness

Serendipitous Beginnings

Everyone has stories about how they met, especially about all the chance encounters, unexpected introductions, and serendipitous coincidences that brought them together. Here are a few of my personal *how we met* stories.

Susan and I met just after I had moved to Florida. I was lecturing at a health food store about why diets don't work. After my talk she came up to me and said, "We have got to know each other!" We chatted for a while and she asked how I liked living here. I blurted out, "I would like it a lot more if I had a women's group for support." Serendipitously, she was putting together just such a group and invited me to join.

Barbara and I met in that women's group, but she seemed so distant at first. Then one day, standing at a mirror combing our hair at the same time, I was complaining about how mine was such a mess that day and she confessed that she felt intimidated by me because I always seemed so perfectly put together and confident. That opening led to all sorts of confessions about our very most real feelings concerning our looks and much more. To this day we honor a commitment to each other to never leave our mirrors before we can see our beauty radiating through, no matter what our inner emotional "chatter" is saying about what we look like at any given moment.

Cynthia and I also met in that group. We became both friends and business partners—cofacilitators of workshops and coauthors of a series of workbooks focused on discovering and navigating life by one's highest values. And so it is that sometimes a new friend opens up a whole new world of possibilities.

Betsy and I met on a tennis court where we were paired up for a friendly game. Afterward, because she had seemed so unhappy and frustrated on the court, I asked her, "You don't seem to enjoy the game at all. Why do you play?" That was the start of a long and intimate conversation that led to a very long friendship.

Ione and I met because she came to my home for a party I was hosting in honor of a mutual friend. While wandering through my house, she caught sight of a dream catcher hanging by my bed. She came looking for me to tell me that she was fascinated by dreams and was paying attention to her own. We decided to meet at sunrise the next day and walk the beach road to share more about the topic. Since then we have been walking the beach at sunrise once a week for more than twenty years.

Patti and I met when we were both visiting a mutual friend in Tennessee for a special celebration. There was a full moon, and I asked those gathered if anyone wanted to take a walk in the moonlight. Patti jumped up immediately and off we went. Although she lives in Los Angeles and I was living in New York City at the time, that night was the beginning of a thirty-something-year deep connection.

As I think back to all these first encounters, I appreciate again just how much of a blessing each of these chance meetings turned out to be. It becomes obvious that we never know when the next great friend will appear in our lives.

Beyond these *beginning* stories, there are all sorts of other marvelous mutual anecdotes that friends cherish together about such varied things as how one friend came to the rescue of the other or how opposites attract or how they are so much alike that they could be siblings or some other wonderfully exhilarating (or difficult) collective experience they will always remember fondly and in great detail.

Discovering and exploring similar as well as diverse experiences or backgrounds is a delightful way to make new friends. How about you? What are your favorite friendship stories about how you made a friend?

Our friendship has been
such an extraordinary journey
from the very beginning
when we first met
I knew I wanted to know you
and to know more about you

from those early conversations
there was so much I appreciated
and admired about you
so much about you that I found
interesting and inspiring
delightful and fascinating
the more I learned
the more I wanted to continue on
our friendship journey

then came the discoveries
of all our intriguing differences
along with a deeper understanding
of our common ground and values
and so our journey expanded

over the years we have enjoyed
many special times together
and so many important experiences
that our friendship has blossomed
and flourished to become a reciprocally
caring exchange of ideas
resources and adventures
and so much love

A Daily Dose of
Friendship

In the world of nutrition, MDR is the abbreviation for the Minimum Daily Requirements of macro- and micronutrients necessary for a healthy body. Borrowing from this concept, how very special and nourishing it is to pay attention to those practices that feed our minds, hearts, and spirits as well.

To think about this another way, consider that MDR can also stand for Mindful Daily Replenishers, Re-energizers, Refreshers, or Restoratives. Whatever word we choose, the idea is that there are certain supportive habits and practices that enrich our lives and allow us to live up to our potential—things like exercise, getting enough sleep, learning something new every day, and making time to slow down and just *breathe*. All these make a difference in the quality of our days and, by extension, our lives.

High on the list of MDRs is taking time each day to connect with a friend. It might be a short phone visit or a longer coffee date or a shared meal or movie or, if we are really lucky and are able to carve out the time, a playdate or weekend visit. Consider friends to be a necessary nutrient—our vitamin F. Anytime is the right time to acknowledge, celebrate, and benefit from the gift of the friendships that nurture us and feed our souls.

like two trees that have grown
side by side
we, too, have grounded our friendship
with deep roots that have intertwined
beneath the surface of things

together we have drawn both sustenance
and inspiration from a common wellspring
ever flowing beneath and between us
and in the proximity
of each other's strong presence
we have each been gifted
with inspiration to reach upward
toward a sky twinkling with starry
dreams worthy of our wishes and our will

like the splendor of all great trees
that connect earth and sky
may the magnificence of our connection
continue to encourage us to reach toward
possibilities that exist in the realm of
what we don't know we don't yet know

Cultivating Friendships in a
Busy and Shifting World

It seems our roots are becoming shallower nowadays as we move from city to city, whether for long- or short-term relocation or because our jobs keep us flying from here to there as we tend to business. Also in today's more mobile world, family and friends are often scattered in all directions. Modern-day links frequently involve cell phones and electronic correspondence with only occasional face-to-face opportunities to reach out and connect with someone, nurture old friendships, or build new ones. While social-networking sites such as Facebook and Twitter offer modern avenues of convenience for staying in touch, it's not enough!

To nurture the friendships you hold dear and to expand your circle of connections, here are some suggestions worth considering:

Be a bit old-fashioned. Schedule time in your day planner each week to meet a friend—either in person or by phone—for a deeply connective half-hour. Or plan some more leisurely time to enjoy with a few best friends.

Multitask in the best sense of the word. Gather some friends together with aprons and bags of groceries to cook up a group dinner. Fill up on both food and friendship. Make conversation while making a meal. Carry on while cleaning up. Another possibility is to make time for a walk 'n' talk with a buddy. What could be better than combining great exercise with great company?

Buddy up when things are tough. Going through a challenge or a crisis? Call on a wise friend who is willing to listen deeply and reflect back to you who you really are: your strengths and talents, your knowledge and intuitive inklings. Spend time "heartstorming" together about the next best steps and possibilities.

Build new bridges. Search out opportunities and networking events to connect with people in your neighborhood, community, and other arenas where you participate, such as a charity, sporting event (yours or your child's), or work/career function. Seek out like-minded others who share an interest in some idea or project you're passionate about.

Find reasons to celebrate. Make an effort to celebrate your friends' milestones and achievements. Make it fun. Make it easy. Make it happen. Support and appreciation are two of the great gifts of friendship, so offer yours.

As Socrates said, "Beware the barrenness of a busy life." Don't allow yourself to be soooo busy that you are left with no time for your friends. Friendships add immeasurably to the richness of our days. With a little imagination and effort, plus some creative time management, you can find ways to stay truly connected, even in this 24/7 on-the-go time we live in. So with whom can you connect today?

*h*ave you gone on a walk 'n' talk lately?
you know...
those lovely connective strolls
or fast-moving, arm-pumping strides
with a friend who is really a friend

it's more about discovering each other
than the terrain covered
whatever the pace
with each in-breath
come ideas and discoveries
questions and explorations
with each out-breath
old outworn attitudes and beliefs
are blown away
just as you, too, are blown away
by newly shared insights or inspirations

what a grand journey it can be
going around the blocks
of the old neighborhood maybe
or along the beach at sunrise
words flying hither and yon
breathtaking vistas and visions
exposed to the light of day
dark caverns of fears and doubts
bravely explored and expunged

what a special sally into the unknown
trees and birds cheering you on
sun smiling or raindrops tapping out
tunes on the sidewalk
while you wander around this grand bazaar
of life's learnings and memories
trading stories and secrets
gathering your findings into your heart
treasures to tuck away
koans to contemplate
ideas to try on
hopes to live with
perhaps even new mantras to live by

what a terrific trip
delightful dalliance
sweet saunter it can be
and certainly worth the journey

Staying Connected and Getting Reconnected

There are those friends with whom we keep in close communication... keeping a finger on the pulse of their lives and even their days. I have four friends with whom I am in contact weekly, sometimes for brief check-ins, other times for long curl-up-on-the-couch chats. Other friends are on my "do not forget list" to remind me to check in every few weeks so as to not lose a significant "beat" in their lives. In addition, for the past ten years I have been involved with two groups of colleagues with whom I have a scheduled monthly teleconference call. We share about our lives, accomplishments, new ideas and projects, as well as anything else that pops up in the course of our hour or more together. All these various deep times of connection are among the most satisfying moments in my life.

On the other hand, catching up with friends, especially those who have drifted away for one reason or another, is like re-entering a river you have visited before. One needs to do so with full presence in the moment. You cannot expect things to be the same as when you last connected... as if their lives stayed frozen in time while yours jogged merrily (or not so merrily) along. It can be slippery and even hazardous to simply assume that all's well or at least in place in exactly the same way that it was last time.

Friendship isn't static and neither are people. Everything and everyone shifts and changes. Recently, I called a friend just to say "hi" after being out of touch for a few months only to find that there had been a death in the family as well as a brand-new business opportunity, the birth of a grandchild, and a personal health challenge in that brief gap since we had last spoken.

Remembering that "Hi! How are you?" need not be a pat question is a great way to begin. Ask and then listen carefully to the response. Don't take "okay" for an answer. Be curious. Ask for details. The more you are willing to be open and receptive, the more you will learn.

I want to confess that finding time for "connectivities" is so important to me that I actually keep a spreadsheet with the names of friends and acquaintances down the left-hand side and twelve monthly columns across the top. That way I can keep tabs on how well I am doing at staying in touch and avoid having those I care about slip through the cracks of my busy life.

a few longtime friends
sitting in a circle
catching up
on the last fifteen years or so
(has it really been that long? we ask
amazed at time's persistent flight)
painting broad brush strokes
across the canvas of our lives

no time or reason to dwell
on the mindless details or minor dramas
swept into forgotten corners
small old sufferings that fall away
rather we attend to the lovely tiny miracles
of living as we disclose
to each other (and ourselves
if truth be told)
how we have arrived
here and now

ah, yes, there have been
the significant others of our lives
the children raised and
sent on their way
careers pursued and jobs left behind
as we climbed the ladder
of our years toward
some higher rung
of fulfillment and satisfaction
and dare we say
joy

because there is most certainly
joy here in this circle
as we share bread and memories
turn by turn
looking back to capture and encapsulate
the broad overview of events
what comes alive in this present moment
is a kind of whimsical acceptance
of self and other
of roads taken or not
of choices made
wise and foolish both

there we were
friends of a certain age
and understanding
gathered around a table
(as friends often do)
finding satisfaction and strength
and sweet solace
in one another's good stories and
good company

this morning, my friend
you wandered into my mind
as casually and easily as if you
had stopped by for a cup of tea
or leaned over the fence to say hello
and I found myself wishing you were here

and so I wanted to reach out to you
across the miles and send you
a long-distance hug
delivered with words on paper rather than arms
and filled with all the love I feel
and appreciation for the gift
of your presence in my life

though we may be separated
by distance and circumstance
when it comes to the times and ways you have
been and continue to be
a dear friend and guiding inspiration
there are no real boundaries between us

I simply wanted to tell you so right now
while you are so fully present here
in my thoughts
with these loving words for you to hold
and save and keep close to your heart
in the days and years to come
as a tangible token of my caring

A Very Personal Friendship Journey

I recently celebrated a milestone birthday and decided to travel the country and visit many dear friends from coast to coast. Beyond simply enjoying one-to-one time with them, my intention was to share privately with each of them (both verbally and in writing) what I most appreciate, love, and celebrate about them while inviting them to do the same for me. The whole experience has been both satisfying and transformative.

The milestone of transitioning into a new decade provided the opportunity to reflect back over the many beautiful years and special moments I have enjoyed, with a particular focus on how each friend's presence in my life shines through as a unique blessing.

Many years ago, I coached a woman who was going through a difficult time and "challenged" her to ask those near and dear to her to express to her what they most appreciated about her. She carried a notebook with her to write down their words *(and if it felt awkward to make the request, she could blame it on her coach!)*. That notebook became a most treasured possession, one which she reread often, especially at times when she needed her spirits bolstered.

So all these years later, I decided to follow my own good advice and invite those who mean the most to me to do the same. What the years have taught me is that it is never too soon to express loving thoughts, because none of us knows when it might be too late. By the way, the impetus for this project was not that I was going through a difficult time. Rather it was quite the opposite; it was a time of many blessings, much gratitude, and a heart full of joy for all that I have had the opportunity to experience and love. All the more reason to seize the moment and acknowledge this milestone passage as positively as possible.

Relationship, defined in positive psychology as *"the capacity to love and be loved,"* is my highest value. So what felt right and appropriate to me was to also present each friend with a handwritten small card with my reflections so they could hold on to my acknowledging words and the feelings they evoked. The impact of these intimate conversations was both beautiful and profound, and in each instance, the experience has now become part of our shared history as friends.

Is there someone whose companionship and friendship you've felt boundless gratitude for along your life's journey? Perhaps *now* is the perfect time to let them know.

*l*et's celebrate
today
like every day
as another anniversary
in the expanding blessing
of our togetherness

counting only the years
of our friendship does not
do justice
to the richness and abundance
of all we have shared
since first we met

every day your name
is in my heart and on my mind
so entwined are we
on this journey of a lifetime

every day I name you
in my list of what I am
most grateful for

every day I speak your name
in my prayers and find
your name showing up
in my journaled reflections

so let's celebrate today

This is a poem that emerged during time spent with a wonderful friend on my several-months-long journey to be in close touch with those I hold most dear. I actually read it to her as we sat beneath the redwoods together.

a quiet stream rippling with sunlight
great redwood trees offering
their presence and grounding
to the two of us here and now
stretched out under their broad
canopy of lush aliveness
bird sounds, children's voices
and even car engines passing by
all part of the moment
and the experience

two friends perched on the roots
of a massive tree that has stood
its own test of time
two friends rooted in a relationship
that has also endured
the onslaught of years and changes
in the weather and more
it doesn't get any better than this
really... it doesn't

two women who have given their all
to their deep connection
who have tended it with time
and attention
with deep caring and the willingness
to honor and celebrate their longtime
love for each other and their long
years of experience
and shared experiences

in the spaciousness
of their sometimes close-by and
sometimes distant proximity
they have offered
to each other again and again
the gifts of openhearted and
true-to-the-bone acceptance
providing both breathing room
and arms to catch each other's fall

with neither judgments nor agendas
with neither assumptions nor fixations
never taking each other
or their friendship
for granted
always there when the going
has gotten rough
such is the blessing of a friendship
allowed to flourish on its own terms

The Value of Relationship

On the grandest of scales, it becomes apparent that everything in life is connected to everything else and our planet exists because of this intricate web. When we are willing to personally acknowledge and honor our own profound connection to that which is beyond our individual selves, we come to deeply experience how it is that we evolve and thrive. Connection to other people is most certainly at the core of what has allowed us to survive and build civilizations—through the sharing of love, hope, ideas, and resources with others and especially with friends.

There are certain values that inspire and motivate us. These high ideals and principles are at the core of what makes us human and humane. As I have explored and named my own values, I have discovered that I place the highest significance on my relationships, particularly those with my friends. Above all else, they are what bring me great happiness and enrich my every day. Arriving at this essential understanding was one of those *aha* moments for me. And once I "got it," my life changed forever. First, I stopped feeling guilty for all the times I put aside whatever business proposal or project I was working on to simply be with a friend—whether to comfort, celebrate, or just hang out for a while. Before my *aha* moment,

I told myself I was wrong for being so easily distracted, for neglecting my endless to-do list, or for slacking off on my drive to accomplish something truly significant (as if tending to relationships is not significant enough).

When I realized how much relationships matter to me, I changed careers and became a life coach, a connective profession if ever there was one.

Being a life coach allows me to witness all the ways that *relationships* are a key aspect to living a fulfilling and meaningful life—one that is worthy of our time, our energy, and our journey here on earth. Whether we build lasting liaisons with two or twenty or two hundred, these are the bonds that matter and make a difference.

take a moment from becoming
a moment just to be
to look through eyes
without a thought
a moment just to see
to break loose of all
the rules we make
a moment to just be free
a moment when the YOU in you
can touch the ME in me

Fluff the Feathers
of Your Friendship

One of the natural outcomes of rewarding relationships is that they become really comfortable and easy over time. That's good news because none of us can be on constant high alert or completely present in each moment indefinitely. It would be exhausting. But the challenge is that, as we ease into the familiarity of someone's companionship, we also slip into the danger zone of taking that same relationship for granted, making the assumption that it will always stay sweet, gratifying, and solid—no matter whether we continue to tend to it quite so lovingly and appreciatively... or not.

Friendships take time and attention, and without both, sooner or later they will wilt from neglect. The metaphor of the proverbial garden requiring care and nurturing comes to mind. Gardens need to be tended to if they are to flourish and continue to yield benefits—both in terms of beautiful flowerings and nutrient-rich foods. We—and our gardens—thrive when kind and loving hands are available.

One way to be thoughtfully available and responsive to valued friends is to remember to make time to simply be with them. Whatever the activity— whether a walk 'n' talk or a fun excursion or meeting over a simple cup of tea—there is no substitute or shortcut for time well spent together. Time is an essential building block in creating the foundation for relationships, especially when you make it apparent how much you enjoy the other person's presence. Good feelings, good understanding, and good memories are made of this. After these opportunities for togetherness, it's also important to actually express how much you enjoyed the pleasure of their company. That way friends take their leave feeling not only seen and heard but refreshed as well. This is not "fluff" (as in superfluous or unnecessary). It is actually at the very core (as in *cœur*, the French word for *heart*) of developing strong and lasting bonds of connection.

Another way to show your gratitude to those you have chosen as friends is to fluff their feathers, so to speak. We all need to feel appreciated for who we are, what we do, and what we bring to our relationships. What better way to shine a spotlight on another than to tell them all that you enjoy and admire about them whenever you have the chance? True compliments are far more than empty or perfunctory platitudes. They let others know that we are paying attention to them, that we notice their virtues and their talents as well as their achievements, and that we are delighted for and proud of them.

While you're at it, you can take your *fluffing* activities one step further by singing your friend's praises any way and where that it seems appropriate. When introducing your buddy to others, be sure to highlight something special about who they are and what they do in the world. Actually, in any group setting, it is always lovely to relate worthwhile accolades and words of appreciation about your friends who are there. And at an event in their honor, be one of the first to stand up and offer a toast or a positive story about him or her. Honest admiration is always a generous and welcome gift. So think about it. Whose feathers can you fluff today?

*Each beautiful shared moment
each time a thought is offered
and received
generously with kindness and grace
each honest exchange of a story
or a secret
each delicate caring touch
each embrace
each possibility for laughter
or tears
each moment of gratitude
each opportunity for intimacy
like feathers placed gently one by one
on a scale
at some magical point in time
tip the scale toward love*

I believe in you
I have known you
through so many ups and downs
and seen you grow
wiser and more resilient
with each experience

I believe in you
I have witnessed
your overflowing generosity
and watched you contribute
to others in ways that matter
and make a difference

I believe in you
I have experienced
the expansiveness of your love
and your enthusiasm for life
along with your determination
to make the world a better place

I believe in you
I have observed
how you listen attentively
and speak authentically
from your own experience
and deep knowing

I believe in you
and every day is the perfect day
for me to tell you how grateful
I am for the gift of your presence
in my life

When I think of you, as I often do
what fills my mind
is a whirlwind of images
detailing all that you miraculously
manage to do and be for others
like a juggler who deftly and
gracefully keeps everything
carefully balanced in the air
all at once without ever missing a beat

when you come to mind, as you often do
what fills my thoughts are
the kindness and enthusiasm
with which you reach out
and embrace life with all
its joys and challenges
like the dancer who steps
into the flow of life's varied music
and swings and sways graciously
so, too, do you dance
with whatever and whomever
shows up on your path

when I hold you in my heart
as I most assuredly do
I am filled with endless
admiration and appreciation
for your presence in the world
and boundless gratitude
for your friendship

Friends Give Each Other the Benefit of the Doubt

Things happen. Life happens. Sometimes it is easy, or at least possible, to loyally show up at all the right times for all the right reasons... and sometimes it is not. Life is complicated. Human beings are complicated. Stuff happens. We all slip and fall. It doesn't mean that we're not doing our best to stay upright.

It's all too easy to jump the gun and open the floodgates to all sorts of snap judgments and opinions about why a friend has somehow let you down—whether it's an appointment cancelled, a birthday missed, a commitment not honored, a confidence betrayed, or whatever else has occurred. But what about when it's you who has disappointed? Maybe you're the one who missed the appointment or forgot the birthday or spoke without first thinking about the ramifications of what you were saying.

The first and best strategy is to stop the mental deluge of negative mind chatter and take a great big generous breath. Then remember that not one of us is without faults or lapses in good judgment. None of us is perfect or perfectly in sync with another at all times. And therein lies a key to forgiveness. We each have blind spots and moments of self-absorption when we forget to take into consideration the needs and feelings of another. When we can recognize and forgive our own blunders and slip-ups, we can begin to make the shift to acceptance and giving another the benefit of the doubt. This nonreactive approach can be both personally restorative and healing for all concerned.

Whatever is going on in your friend's world is about them—their attitudes, beliefs, choices, and judgments—it's not about you. And the same is true for you—your friend can't always know what is going on in your life at any given moment. It's when you can shift your perspective to accept that fact, when you can dig deep and find your own munificence of spirit to accept and forgive, that you can turn your thoughts toward gratitude for all the beautiful ways your friend has and does show up in your life and vice versa. By expanding your open-heartedness, you can find your way to a point of genuine understanding.

Slipping out of gratitude
can be all too easy
a fear here
a disappointment there
and I notice that I have lost
my sure footing
on the well-worn
surface of thankfulness

sliding away from peace
can be disturbingly easy
a disruption here
a drama there
and I find that I have
released my firm grip
on serenity in exchange for
desperate displays of restless upset
and moments of imbalance

yet what I know about
slipping and sliding
is how the sure grip
of a friend's hand
or their listening ear
can arrest my precipitous
fall from grace
can refocus my teeter tottering
mind and once again
center me in love

two oddly matched friends
longtime companions
through countless years
and tears and cheers
who have journeyed together
along the peaks
and valleys and sometimes level
expanses of lives fully lived

two familiar travelers
who have found it necessary
from time to time
to create a certain spaciousness
between their periods of togetherness
so different were they
in perspective and temperament
that their proximity
would border on claustrophobic
becoming disconcerting perhaps
or too difficult

and yet there remained
always there, always flowing
even through the separations
of the between times
a deep wellspring of love
and compassion
uniting these women
no matter their dissimilarities

so much so that again and again
forgiveness created a well-worn path
back into each other's lives
so much so that
on the simultaneous occasion
of their many-decade milestone birthdays
no matter the periodic
gaps in communication
there arrived at each other's door
a lovingly chosen gift
perfectly in harmony
with that woman's essence
selected with the utmost care
certain to evoke that satisfying
smile of pleasure
reserved for one who knows another
profoundly well

Make New Friends

I have always wondered about the song lyrics, "Make new friends, but keep the old. One is silver, and the other is gold." Yes, I certainly believe in the value of longtime friendships and cherish their presence in my life. Still, there is something to be said about the absolute delight and importance of always continuing to make new friends. And who is to say that one is more valuable than the other?

Each new friend represents an unknown universe of ideas, experiences, and perspectives—a virtual treasure chest of shiny new possibilities. But we tend to balk at the idea of networking in a room full of unfamiliar faces or arriving at a party where we don't feel connected to or even known by the group that has gathered. Yet life often requires that we somehow bite the bullet, find our courage, and walk into that den of at-the-moment strangers. I say "at-the-moment," because a stranger is nothing more than someone whom you don't yet know.

Here's a useful trick—a shift in mindset actually— that can make all the difference in how you approach situations in which you are not already acquainted with all those present. I like to call this the "treasure hunt" approach. Simply make the assumption that everyone you have the opportunity to meet has some fascinating story to tell, some thought-provoking experience or point of view worth knowing about, or some common link, connection, or interest worth uncovering. Then just be curious. Ask questions that go beyond the ordinary social protocols of name, rank, and serial number (or, more likely, job, profession, and title). Inquire about what made their day memorable, what grabbed their interest, or what made them smile or laugh out loud. Use any excuse necessary: "I am doing a personal research project on joy" *(certainly a worthy use of your time)* or "I am involved in marketing and like to observe what people pay attention to" *(we are all always marketing ourselves)* or "I am intrigued by what makes life special to others" *(aren't we all?)*. You can even just fess up and say that you are on a treasure hunt to meet and find out about interesting people and wanted to take advantage of this opportunity.

Treasure hunting for new acquaintances, who may eventually become new friends who may eventually become old friends, is something we "get" to do. It's not meant to be an arduous or awkward chore. As humans, we have the capacity to communicate ideas, and it is in our DNA to want to know and know about others. It truly is magical just how many ways there are for new friends to serendipitously appear in our lives... *if* we are willing to take notice.

let's be friends
it doesn't matter that we just met
ideas are birthed in an instant
and the course of history
has been changed by a conversation
more than once

so why not simply decide
right here and now
that we shall be friends
indeed that we shall be steadfast friends
kind and attentive
listening well and learning
from each other
enjoying each other's agreeable
company and fine qualities
savoring this unexpected
good fortune of having met

it's not every day
that two people who were
so recently strangers
get to spend such a delightful hour
so open-mindedly and open-heartedly
and enthusiastically alive with each other
turning away from potential
distractions and disturbances
to explore the potential of the moment
and simply breathe in
each other's presence

let's not just exchange stuff
like names and numbers
let's exchange a commitment
to companionship
to remaining curious
to staying linked
indeed to building a bridge
of ongoing connective moments
that is fortified by our delight
in this chance to truly know
each other

today is just the beginning
if we let it be

Familiarity

Something that is interesting about new friendships is that often there is a certain underlying familiarity about people we are meeting for the first time, as if we have encountered each other on some level before. There is that sense of an almost subliminal connection.

One day I was sitting in a circle at a workshop on mindfulness meditation. Each of those present took a turn sharing something about themselves and what brought them to this program. Afterwards, thinking about all that I heard, I wrote this poem of acknowledgment.

I know your story
perhaps not the details
and particulars, of course
but I have heard the essence
of your experience come whistling
across my own lips
have witnessed it tumbling
out in my own waves of enthusiasm
or enfolded in my own heaving
sighs of grief
or tremors of fear

I know your journey
perhaps not the precise dates
or places, of course
but I can recognize certain essential
elements because they resemble those
woven into my own rites of passage
with multiple variations, of course
changes in tempo or intensity or theme
but still with basic undertones intact
complete with the inevitable high
and low notes and reverberations

joy, sadness, hope, despair
loneliness, love, lassitude
exasperation, excitement
grit and gratitude
all those same complex
and contradictory elements echoing
through the unique composition
of my own experiences

and so it is that my heart
can break wide open
to the sound of your voice
the shape of your words
the telling of your narrative

and so it is that I can
feel your happiness
and sense your sorrow
and hold them tenderly, respectfully
prayerfully, sacredly
as my own

In Praise of
Authenticity

Holding back our true selves, even just a little, leaves a palpable gap that keeps us separated from the deep connection for which we yearn. When we are tempted to appear to be more than (or even worse, *better than*) someone else, it opens up a chasm of judgments and righteousness that can lure even the best of us, in a momentary descent into small-mindedness, into a precipitous downfall. And what is also true is that we become *less* in the process.

It is only when we can love ourselves whole just the way we are, only when we can show up with our bumps and bruises, our shadowy fears and gloomy disappointments, that we can open our hearts enough to also love others in ways that they can experience our good intentions and our love. Ultimately, it is our honest acceptance of who they are and how they are, however *that* is, that allows for a bridge to form across the place of our disappointments and differences.

Truth be told, less is more. Our real, uninflated selves are far more appealing than any pretenses and postures we might want to feign in order to impress someone. And one true gesture, initiated from the heart, is all it takes to expansively traverse the distance between love and the fear that arises when we feel that we may be less than enough just the way we are.

let's be real
let's not waste precious minutes
squirming around in the labyrinths
of posturing and pretending

let's be true
let's show up
open and vulnerable
with free spirits and unfettered minds
full of boundless curiosity

let's give our best selves
over to candid encounters
made splendid by sincere
pauses for deep connection

anything less than
astounding authenticity
is wasteful and exhausting
for all concerned

what is lost is far more than
just minutes which are indeed
precious but not nearly
so much so as our truest selves

let's join together instead
for a truly gratifying and overflowing
cup of deliciously honest
conversational tea

Best Friends

I remember when I was young the importance of having a best friend—one person with whom to play and share secrets and join forces to face the world with all its confusing ups and downs, rules and messages, demands and limitations, choices and roadblocks, and so much more.

I remember as well how hurtful it was when, for whatever reason, something changed or snapped and we were no longer "besties"—our allegiances had shifted. Those were the black and white years when the concept of more than one best friend was, by definition, an impossibility.

Fortunately as we mature our perspectives widen and fortuitous circumstances allow us to gather new friends as we roll along, broadening our horizons and understanding. As our hearts expand to embrace first one new friend and then another, we begin to appreciate that perhaps love has no boundaries and to realize that the need to create a rank order of likes and dislikes is both unnecessary and inappropriate. There's room enough in our life song for lots and lots of friendship notes, with each one in its own unique way contributing to a richer and more beautiful melody.

*t*here are thresholds of realness
moments on the mind maps
we use as we navigate life
crossing over points in time
when we no longer hold back
our most honest selves

there are moments of truth
so poignant and raw
when we finally unveil the essence
of our most real selves
and our truest yearnings

there are vistas of hope
beyond those barriers
of our own making
when we finally allow
our full aliveness
to break through

and then at last
we are able to rely upon those who
like us
are finding their footing
along that same road to realness
others who are willing to meet
our gaze because they, too
face the difficulties
and possibilities we all share

The Gift of Breaking Bread

It is difficult to write about connection and gathering with friends without also writing about food. Most certainly, since the beginning of time, people have gathered to share meals. Whether we come together for an ordinary repast or to celebrate a special occasion, food is part and parcel of both familial and communal occasions.

There is much that happens when we break bread together, and so it is that our dining tables are often at the very epicenter of our friendships. When we take the time to settle in, we create the spaciousness to savor more than just the tastes and aromas and satisfy more than our basic hunger. Good conversation, thoughtful exchanges of ideas, and proper appreciation and acknowledgment of others who are present offer sustenance and nourish us just as surely as do the macro- and micronutrients present on our plate. Whether we are cooking and serving or simply gratefully receiving the loving efforts of others, the exchange fills our hearts and minds as well as our bellies.

In today's very busy world where all too many things, including grabbing something to eat, happen on the run, it is more important than ever to make time to set a table, sit down, and break bread together.

We begin
with certain protocols of greeting
whether handshakes or hugs
warm smiles or reverent bows
we are welcomed
into the space of another
genially, cordially
graciously

once settled in
feeling at ease and perhaps
comfortably at home
we might open ourselves further
to simple offerings of hospitality

from candles that are lit
to the sounds of ritual blessings
intoned like mantras
awakening us to the core
to the breaking of bread and
the comforting foods lovingly served
by those whose heartstrings
reverberate with ours

long, slow, sweet, cozy hours later
our time together at an end
we are satisfied beyond food
beyond measure and beyond boundaries
we say our goodbyes soulfully
with a sense of belonging
that is sacred

True Community

Authentic community is that spaciousness where we can speak freely without having to edit our words or curb our passions. It is the place where we feel most warmly welcomed, embraced, and celebrated for who we are. Its foundation is one of love, respect, trust, and the quality time necessary for those cornerstones to rise up.

Still, it is important to recognize that we have choices about where and with whom we establish our strongest roots and connections. What I'm sure about is this: we each need to seek out and celebrate those with whom we can be open, authentic, and free. The quality of our days and the fullness of our lives depend on the success of this ongoing search for real friendship.

Taking this idea to the next level, sometimes there are small bands of friends who are committed to one another in some especially deep and abiding way. I actually belong to a "tribe." That's what we call ourselves. We are a group of life coaches who began coming together on a regular basis simply to share ideas and best practices. That was ten years ago, and at some point we recognized and acknowledged that we were far more than just a group of colleagues. We were indeed a tribe in the best sense of the word—loyal and sincere and committed to one another. We know one another's families and stories and challenges and sweet successes. We have been there for one another to celebrate all sorts of good happenings—large and small. And we have been there for one another through surgeries, crises, divorces, financial issues, and more. When the wife of one of our tribal members was diagnosed with breast cancer, WOW did we ever rally fast. All it took was one e-mail letting us know. I happened to be sitting at my computer at the time, and within minutes we started showing up, one and all, with information and resources and offers to be at the hospital and wherever else we might be needed. By the way, while we all live in Florida, we are scattered all over the state. So we also immediately formed a virtual prayer circle. Every night at 9 p.m. our phone alarms were set to go off so that we could all simultaneously turn our attention to sending healing thoughts in the direction of the woman in need.

Do you have a tribe? Call it a clan, a family of choice, an intimate community—we all need one. Make it a priority to build and acknowledge these foundational relationships that can make all the difference.

In this world
of not enoughness
where there is always
something more to do
something more to become
your great gift to me
is seeing myself
reflected in your eyes
where loving acceptance
shines a holy light
upon my soul

in this world
of more is better
where there is always
something more to possess
something more to achieve
may my great gift to you
be that you feel me always
holding you
in all your imperfect splendor
with abundant gratitude
for your presence
in my life

in this world
of constant striving
where there appears to always be
someone more worthy
someone more perfect
may our great gift to each other
be that we embrace
again and again
our divinity
yours and mine
as we hold each other
with hands
and hearts
as we celebrate
the gifts we are
in this world

Friends Connect Each Other to the Larger World

To connect means literally to bind or fasten. It involves bringing together seemingly separate entities and creating a bond or link between them. From the beginning, even before the time of recorded history, people have come together for company and safety; for solace and celebration; and to share knowledge, insights, and wisdom. Together we have explored, questioned, and tested the boundaries of our capacity to be fully human. At the river's edge, around the campfire, during rites of passage that span giving birth, initiations into adulthood, death, and everything in between, we have gathered together.

At our best, there is something within us that recognizes we are each part of something much larger than ourselves—part of the family of man. And yet there are times when we shut ourselves off from others, allowing ourselves to put up barriers based on our differences rather than bridges built upon our common humanity. Friends help us to reconnect in positive and cooperative ways with the larger communities all around us. They offer opportunities to join with others in ways that kindle our vitality and spark our sense of purpose and true belonging.

how wonderful it is that
no matter our mother tongue
we as humans can communicate
friendship and caring
concern and cooperation
with nothing more than a true smile
and open arms poised
to welcome another
to our hearths and hearts

how hopeful it is that
no matter our ingrained ways
of working and playing and praying
we as citizens of this life-sustaining planet
are most certainly capable
of offering our respect and appreciation
for worldviews and vistas
and best practices that differ vastly
from our own

how encouraging it is that
no matter our unique paths and purposes
we all share hopes
for love and safety
for comfort and contribution
as we each seek to find
our way into the fullness
of this life we have been given

Considering that we are
none of us wise enough
or strong enough or clever
or creative enough alone
how considerate and necessary
it is that we remember
time and again
to turn to one another
with gratitude and respect

considering the ways that we are
each of us so interdependent
on one and another
our lives so interwoven
down to the details and intricacies of
our everyday goings and doings
that something as simple
as putting food on our table
or even simply setting a place
or more simply still
seeding a garden or field
requires the work and wisdom
of thousands of hands and tools
and practices that stretch back
to the beginnings of time
even to the harnessing of fire
the weaving of baskets
and the discovery of the wheel

while we as humans have collectively
scaled the highest peaks and soared
way into the heavens
reached far into the depths
of oceans and delved into
the magnificent complexities
of our own bodies and minds
not one of us
could have done any such thing
on our own

and so it is that we must truly be
forever and always beholden
beyond measure to those
upon whose shoulders we stand
those who came before and those
who journey with us now

and what is ours to do in this
and every moment
with great humility
and even greater awe
is quite simply to remember
and give thanks

Friends Inspire Us

Often we are drawn to our friends because of who they are at their core. From the moment they first come into our presence, even from across the room, they radiate a certain essential authenticity and depth of character that attracts us and arouses our curiosity. We want to know them, to know about them, and to spend time with them.

Over time, these friends become the loyal companions who inspire us to step more fully into our own authenticity. They bring out the best in us. They are the patient gardeners who, year after year, encourage our souls to blossom. No matter where life takes us, no matter if our paths diverge at times, still we carry a bit of their radiant spark within us to light the way.

This is especially true when things get difficult. I am reminded of the beautiful observation made by Albert Schweitzer as he reflected about friendship: "Sometimes our light goes out but is blown into flame by another human being. Each of us owes deepest thanks to those who have rekindled this light." A veritable friend is certainly aware of our weaknesses but still and always recognizes and reminds us of our strengths. They sense our fears and anxieties but stand by us and steadfastly encourage us to move beyond these trepidations. When we are lost in a dark sea of hopelessness, these kind and caring companions are the ones who remind us of what is still possible.

When the storms hit
and the winds blow
with fierce abandon
how comforting to know
that no matter our physical
distance I am held
ever so firmly in your heart

your concern reaches
across the miles and
wraps me in a warm and
comforting cloak
reminding me that no matter
the circumstances I am sheltered
during these turbulent nights
and blustery days
by your love and friendship
all around me

You inspire me...
   the way you approach
each day with possibility
on your mind
and hope in your heart
bringing your enthusiasm for life
to all that you are and
all that you do

you inspire me...
the way you walk toward life
with open arms
and an open attitude
ready to embrace whatever
comes your way

you inspire me...
the ways you accept
opportunities and challenges alike
with a can-do courage
choosing your next best steps
with passion and purpose

you inspire me...
your capacity for being
so alive and present
in each and every moment
neither weighed down by regrets
nor wasting time
wishing for impossibilities

you inspire me...
your authenticity and capacity
for joy and celebration
your ability to engage in life
with strength and spirit
and a whole lot more

In the Spirit of Friendship...

I read somewhere that a good friend is an elixir for the soul. An elixir is a potion or preparation that can nurture vitality, energy, and health. And so, what I wish for us all is that throughout our lives we may each be blessed with good friends and the capacity to recognize and celebrate them... and to celebrate life with them.

In that same spirit, what I wish for each of us is that we continually tap into our own capacity to be a loyal friend to others as well as to ourselves. May we find ways to treasure our friendships and honor them with a fullness of heart and a lightness of being. This gift of friendship in all its manifestations is at the core of living an abundantly joyful life and of flourishing.

Friendship changes us. It empowers us to shift our focus beyond that which might be negative or upsetting, isolating or depleting, to the blessings of honest caring, true kindness, and a deep sense of belonging.

Wishing you joy
and bright shiny days
filled with kindnesses
given and received
love that plays on your heartstrings
and sweet time to enjoy
each melody

wishing you laughter
and easy hours
with plenty of time
for peace and contentment
as well as chances
to indulge in your most playful
and silliest of impulses

wishing you happiness
and fulfilling years,
brimming with the success
and satisfaction that comes
from work well done
friendships nurtured
and the grace and gratitude
that enriches it all

What readers have to say about
Friendship Is a Journey...

Coach Minx has deep reserves of wisdom, insight, and compassion, which she shares generously in this book. As a clinical psychologist, I have read many books about relationships, but few possess the warmth and lucid prose of this one. I believe readers will be enlightened and delighted and want to recommend it to and gift it to friends.

Tova Wein, PhD

Love it! Terrific and heartwarming book. Just like cuddling up on the sofa sipping tea with a cozy quilt wrapped around me, talking intimately with a best friend. What a contribution Minx Boren has given to the world.

Gayle A. Landen, President,
Landen, Wells & Associates, Strategic Change Consultants

The beauty and wisdom in this "gift" of a book is profound. Give it to a friend. Give it to lots of friends. Give it to anyone who wants to live a good life. The essays and poems are accessible and inspiring. I love this book! Thank you, Minx Boren, for writing it.

Ayn Fox, MCC, Catalyst at Creativity Lab

Friendship Is a Journey is so full of love, joy, and compassion that you will want to share it with your friends as much as I do. It is an extraordinary book, beautifully written and filled with tender stories and insightful wisdom. What makes this book so special is that no matter where you are in life, no matter how perfect or imperfect your relationships may be, this book is a wonderful reminder that love and opportunities for deep connection are all around us. Minx's extraordinary book opens our eyes to the undiscovered possibilities and magical connections that are the promise of every single day.

Valerie Ramsey, Author of Creating What's Next: Gracefully